Toxic Relationships

7 Signs That You Are In A Toxic Relationship

Introduction

I want to thank you and congratulate you for downloading the book, *"7 Signs That You Are In A Toxic Relationship"*.

This book contains proven steps and strategies on how to recognize the various signs of a toxic relationship and why you need to get out of it. The hardest relationships to get out of are often the most dysfunctional. Life has a bigger plan for you with happiness, health and stability. The book provides guidance as a coach, therapist and a friend.

Thanks again for downloading this book, I hope you enjoy it!

Contents

Chapter 5 – Smart Techniques for Handling Toxic People

Chapter 6 – Strategies for Dealing with Toxic People

Chapter 1

What is a toxic relationship?

Human beings are created for relationships. All of us long for connection with a special one. Toxic means deadly, poisonous or damaging and when you are in a toxic relationship, it can damage your self-esteem and poison your life.

A toxic relationship by definition, is a relationship that is characterized by behavior on the part of the toxic partner this is emotionally and at times, physically damaging to their partner. Toxic relations may exist not just between partners, but also between coworkers, friends and family members.

Most human relations begin with excitement, hope, anticipation and optimism. The thought of two people falling in love and building a life together can be exhilarating. All this changes when you have an unhealthy relationship.

The expectations and needs of one or both partners are subject to change during the course of a relationship. When people hold on to unrealistic expectations they may be unable to identify the toxic changes in their relationship.

Signs of a toxic relationship are not always easy to spot. Although physical violence and infidelity may be signs that are easy to spot, there are other subtle signs that most people involved in such relationships tend to miss.

Do you feel that you are losing your peace of mind or your identity in a relationship? You may not realize this, but you may be in the middle of a relationship that is toxic for your self-esteem and health. The sad fact is that you are not even aware that you are in an unhealthy relationship.

Are you in a relationship where you feel more tired and stressed instead of happy? You may unknowingly be trapped in a relationship that makes you angry, depressed, sad and leaves you so completely drained that you do not have the strength to get out of it.

Toxic relationships may come in different hues. Toxic people are all around us and sometimes they may be in the form of our loved one and at other times they may be our family and friends.

When you are in a toxic relationship, it may seem as if you cannot do anything right. When you are constantly put down, you start believing that you are no good. You feel ashamed of yourself. Although you feel unsettled and uncomfortable, you lack the confidence and will to step out of a relationship that you know is not good for you.

Toxic behavior is a powerful form of manipulation in which people close to us manipulate our feelings either directly or indirectly. These people know how much we value our relationship with them and use our vulnerabilities to shape their threats.

How do many capable and smart people fall victim to toxic behavior? One of the main reasons is that the toxic person makes it truly difficult to see that they are manipulating you. The manipulation is so obscure that you hardly notice what is happening.

Questionnaire to Identify Toxic Relationships

- Do you feel energized or drained after you spend time with your loved one?

- Do you constantly feel sorry for yourself?

- Are you consistently disappointed with the behavior of your partner?

- Are you always giving more to the relationship than your partner?

- Is your relationship painful and confusing?

- Are you comfortable expressing yourself to your partner?

- Does your partner use threats of force or violence to make you do things that you do not want to do?

- Does your partner humiliate you in public and in front of family and friends?

- Do you feel afraid of your partner?

- Are you intimidated in their presence?

- Are you scared to disagree with your partner?

- Are you allowed to make any decisions in your relationship?

- Are you able to freely express your thoughts and feelings with your partner?

- Do you feel lonely in your relationship?

- Do you feel that you are less intelligent and less qualified when you are around this person?

- Do you feel angry and irritable after interacting with them?

- Does your partner make you feel disgusted?

- Do you feel drained of your physical and emotional energy in the presence of this person?

- Are you confused and have difficulty concentrating when you are with this toxic individual?

- Do you experience sharp mood swings when interacting with this individual?

We all want to feel loved, happy and safe in a relationship, but this is not always the case. Most times the red flags of a bad relationship are not too obvious and we do not pay attention to them. This can be a big mistake.

Although some type of bickering is good for a relationship, if you are constantly fighting, it is a big sign that something is bad. Such relationships are negative and unhealthy. The negativity can impact all aspects of your life and can affect your health too.

Most people are blind to the reality that they are caught in a toxic relationship. Even when they become aware of this reality they hold on the relationship with the hope that the other person may change their behavior for good.

It is advisable to confront your toxic relationship instead of trying to deny it or brushing it aside. When you confront this reality, you may be able to make the necessary changes to your lifestyle and personality.

When you hold on to a damaging relationship, it can prevent personal growth. Walking away shows courage and personal strength. Always remember that you are worth more than a toxic relationship. Gain knowledge about the different types of toxic relationships and how they can affect you.

Most of the time it may be hard to tell if you are in a toxic relationship, if you are in it for long. Before you start blaming yourself, you need to remember that such relationships do exist and the signs are often so subtle that you miss them completely.

Confidence, strength and the support of loved ones may enable you to get out of a toxic relationship. Remember that you must make an effort after you identify the signs. It may be difficult to accept that the person you love may not be the right one for you.

Signs You Are in A Toxic Relationship

- **Fighting Constantly** – Fighting is common in any relationship but if you are constantly fighting and arguing with each other, you need to take a closer look at your relationship.

- **Feeling Drained** – If instead of feeling happy and content, you are always physically and emotionally drained, it can be a sign of toxic relationship.

- **Constantly Unhappy** – Does the person in your life constantly make you unhappy? Life with a loved one is supposed to be happy but if you are always unhappy and withdrawn, you need to give a serious thought to your future with this person.

- **Emotional Abuse** – Does your partner belittle and insult you on purpose so that they can feel better? When you are emotionally abused, you may lose your confidence and self-esteem.

- **Physical Abuse** – This should not be acceptable under any circumstances. This is a sure sign of an unhealthy relationship. In this situation one individual is trying to keep the other person under control by intimidating them and using physical force as a tool to accomplish what they want.

- **Insecure** – Do you feel safe with your partner? If you are always afraid of what they may say or do, you may be insecure in the relationship.

- **Blame Game** – If your partner blames you for everything and refuses to take responsibility for their actions, it is a sign of a negative relationship.

The trickiest aspect about toxic relationships is that they do not start toxic. They usually start as exciting and fun and within no time turn toxic. As the signs are subtle you fail to notice when things have started going awry and by the time realization dawns, you are already feeling miserable.

Most people in a toxic relationship find themselves in a situation that they do not want to be but unfortunately, find themselves stuck in it. Although you may not have power over the situation, remember that you still have control over it. Whatever happens or has happened in your life, you deserve better.

Toxic individuals are:

- Controlling and manipulative

- Narcissistic and negative

- Demanding

- Extremely insecure

- Abusive

- Competitive and over-the-top perfectionists

- Cheats and liars

- Bitchy and jealous

Irrespective of how hard you try, you may never be able to satisfy a toxic individual. They will always find fault with whatever you do. You need to understand that everything in life is about them and it is never about you. You become so lost and confused that you forget that you have a life of your own.

If you are not sure that you are in a toxic relationship, you can choose to keep a diary. This can help you get a reality check on the situation. The diary can enable you to collect evidence about actions and words that have caused deep anger and resentment in you.

When you are in a toxic relationship your self-esteem plunges to new lows. The situation becomes extremely bad when you start blaming and hating yourself for everything and become overwhelmed with guilt.

Stop feeling helpless, as you can still turn a bad situation around. Remember that you can always control your actions and reactions. Be honest with yourself and accept the fact that you are in a relationship with a toxic individual. When you acknowledge the fact that you are in a bad relationship you may be able to save further pain.

Chapter 2

Types of Toxic Relationships

1. Controller

One of the most obvious signs of a toxic relationship is when your partner is always controlling. It is as if they are trying to control your every move. No one wants to be told what to do and how to do it all the time. A person that truly loves you will never put you on a leash. It is like walking on eggshells.

When was the last time you made a choice on your own? Controlling does not have to be physically violent or threatening. You may be so frightened that you may be afraid to freely share your views and opinions about anything. Are you afraid and withdrawn in your relationship?

You are afraid of your partner's emotional reaction, as you know that whatever you say may be ignored or overruled. One person calls all the shots and the other simply gives in. The relationship is not on an equal footing as one has all the power and the other doesn't.

2. Belittler

In this type the toxic individual always belittles you by making fun of everything you do. Anything that you say and do is stupid and silly. They will not hesitate to belittle you in front of family, friends and in public.

Even when you have asked them to stop such behavior they continue to indulge in it and often disguise it in various ways. "Can't you take a joke or I am just kidding", is the most common ways of disguising things.

The problem is that it is not a joke and they are not kidding. They want to have complete decision making power and if you tolerate such behavior long enough, you lose your self-esteem.

3. Bad Temper

If you have given up on disagreeing or arguing with your partner as you are worried about their bad temper, it is a classic behavioral trait of the toxic person. They want to control by intimidating you. These individuals have an unpredictable temper and you are never sure what triggers the bad temper.

A surprising aspect about such emotionally abusive individuals is that they never show this side of their self to the outside world. Most often they come across as easy going and pleasant in public.

If you ever confront them about their bad temper they may blame the outburst on you. It is always your fault that they are angry and you are the reason they scream and yell. They disown any responsibility for this behavior.

4. Guilt Inducer

A toxic relationship need not be just between two individuals in a committed relationship, it can also be between family members and friends. The control in such relationships is exercised by inducing guilt. You are made to feel guilty anytime you do something that the guilt inducer does not like.

The most interesting aspect about such people is that they may use others to convey their hurt or sense of disappointment to you. In a family, the mother may make use of the father to convey her disappointment about the son or daughter.

They keep you in control not just by inducing guilt but also be removing it temporarily, if you do what they want you to do. Any guilt prone individual may want the guilt to be removed and this gives the guilt inducer absolute control and power.

5. Deflector and Overreactor

If you have ever tried telling your partner that you are hurt and unhappy about what they said and did but find yourself taking care of their unhappiness and hurt, you may be dealing with a toxic overreactor.

Instead of getting comfort you are always comforting them. You feel bad that you are so selfish and that your behavior had upset your partner.

6. Over Dependent Partner and Independent Controller

One method of toxic control is to be so passive that you want all decisions to be taken by your partner. All decisions without exception need to be taken by you so that you are responsible for everything. Passivity is a very powerful way to control.

If you are in a relationship with an over-dependent partner, you may experience fatigue and anxiety as you are constantly worried about making a wrong decision. You become emotionally drained, as you have to make all the decisions in your relationship.

Such individuals disguise their toxic behavior by asserting their independence. They rarely keep their commitments and control you by keeping you in the dark about what they may do. The anxiety that you feel in such relationships can affect your physical and mental health.

As their behavior is completely unpredictable you do not feel safe and secure in a relationship with them. You are not sure whether the relationship is a priority with them and whether they are emotionally connected with you.

7. Users and Possessive Nature

When you start a relationship with a user they seem completely nice and courteous individuals. As long as they get what they want, they continue to remain this way. In such a relationship, you are always made to feel that you have not done enough for them. As you are constantly trying to do more, you are drained of all energy.

If you are in a relationship with an individual who is possessive, then that is definitely bad news. These individuals are not just jealous, but also too controlling. They become more and more suspicious with the passage of time and may start interrogating you for everything you do. This can make your life miserable.

They may not allow you to have any kind of meaningful relationship with anyone including your family and friends. You may cease to have a life of your own as everything that you do is viewed with suspicion.

Toxic relationships are not limited to your partner. You may have a toxic relationship with a family member, friend, colleague and boss. The other important thing that you need to remember that these relationships are not gender specific. The toxic individual may be a man or a woman.

Most people in a toxic relationship go through an emotional roller coaster ride. You never know when you may feel up and when you may go down. There is a lot of uncertainty associated with such relationships.

When you are in an unresolved toxic relationship, it can gradually wear down your body and cause a lot of emotional stress. You may be surprised to know that your emotional health can have a big effect on your physical body.

A toxic relationship can make you chronically angry, frustrated, frightened and tired. Remember that any kind of abusive relationship can be considered toxic. Power struggles are common in such relationship, as one individual always wants to have the upper hand and dominate all aspects without the other person having any kind of say in it.

Even when you spend time with your loved one you feel lonely. It is as if you feel trapped in their presence. In an attempt to constantly please your partner, you have lost your true self. You are no longer the person you used to be.

Chapter 3

Toxic Relationships in Families

Toxic families are a sad fact. Negative family members can cause a lot of stress and can have an adverse effect on your health and wellbeing. Criticism, manipulation, jealousy, envy, neediness and other such negative traits not just drain you emotionally but also make you feel bad about yourself.

Signs You Are Dealing with Toxic Family Members

Most of us are not sure whether we are dealing with a toxic family member. We think that it is all in our head and that we are just overreacting to their antics. Due to this we tend to ignore things and do not react until the anxiety and stress of dealing with it starts affecting our health directly.

1. **Feeling Angry, Sad and Down Around Them**

   No matter what you say or do, they always say and do things that make you feel bad about yourself. Each time you say no to anything they want you to do they make you feel guilty.

A lot of times they make comments that may not attack you directly but are specifically said to make you feel bad. They always come up with ways to make you feel ashamed, guilty, hurt and resentful.

You may be so stressed that just the thought of interacting with them may make you feel angry and you may start avoiding them.

2. Constant State of Need

All of us are perfectly capable of taking care of our individual needs. If a family member has a constant state of need and want you to take care of all your needs, it can lead to a situation where you lose your individuality.

When you are forced to treat an adult like a child and take care of all their problems, it is a sign that you are dealing with a toxic family member who does not want to take any responsibility.

3. Feeling Drained

When you are around your loved ones, you feel happy and energetic. They make you feel great about yourself. But when you are with toxic family members, you may feel drained and exhausted. Your energy level is down and you do not feel like doing anything.

4. Feel Numb and Sad

You feel alive and happy when you are around people you love. If you feel sad and numb and just go through the motions when you are with a family member, it is an indication that you are in an unhealthy relationship.

You are emotionally drained and do things that you are obligated to do without feeling happy. It is usually a sign that the family member around you is controlling. You shut down your emotions and do things so that you do not upset anyone.

5. Unable to Express Yourself

When you are unable to express your thoughts and feelings freely to a family member because you have to be careful about what you can say to them, it is a sign of a toxic relationship. It is as if you are walking on eggshells and need to be careful about each word you speak.

6. They Control the Relationship

All relationships need to be built on mutual respect and love. Relationships that are on equal footing tend to thrive and are successful. When one person controls all aspects of the relationship, it is an unhealthy one and doomed to fail.

They decide what you need to do, say and whom you can interact. When one person has the upper hand all the time, you start feeling resentful.

7. Feeling Completely Different Around Them

When you feel that you just can't be yourself when you are around a family member and need to curtail your normal behavior, it is a sign of an unhealthy relationship. You behave completely different when you are around them.

If the toxic behavior of a family members becomes physical, it needs to be addressed immediately. Although it is hard, you need to take action against such behavior as it can be dangerous if left unchecked.

Most people who suffer from a toxic family relationship find it hard to maintain a normal relationship. As their self-esteem is already low they are afraid of committing to a healthy relationship.

How to Deal with Toxic Family Members

It may be easy to get rid of a toxic friend, colleague or boss, but how do you get rid of a family member? Toxic family members can include parents, siblings and other relatives. Ending a family relationship is not easy.

Avoid making impulsive and hasty decisions that you might regret later. This can add to your guilt and make it easier for the toxic individual to manipulate you for their gains. If the very thought about the family member makes you feel sick and angry, it is big clue that the relationship has become unhealthy.

Evaluate Your Relationship

Take time to think. If you have decided to end a family relationship immediately after a major fight or heated argument or too many critical remarks, you need to cool down first. Take a deep breath and evaluate the relationship.

Is the relationship really important to you? How will the other family relationships get affected if you decide to end this one? Are there any positives associated with this relationship? How long have you been suffering in silence?

- **Abuse** – If you have been suffering from any kind of verbal, emotional and physical abuse, it may be time to call it quits. You do not have to worry about the possible fallout as your safety and security is of utmost importance. Physical abuse should never be tolerated as it can cause grievous injury to your body.

- **Affects Other Areas of Your Life** – Is the negative situation having an adverse effect on other areas of your life? Does it affect your sleep, performance at work and personal relationship with others? If you have answered "Yes", you need to walk away.

- **Negative Interactions Only** – All relationships go through ups and downs but if yours is only negative, you need to look closely at it. Do your parents only criticize you? Do your siblings start an argument each time you are in their presence? Are you constantly arguing and fighting over petty issues?

-

  If there is nothing positive about your toxic family member, you need to decide whether you truly need them in your life. If having them or not having them does not make any kind of difference to you, it is time to move on as quickly as possible.

- **One Sided** – Healthy relationships are based on give and take. If your toxic family member never reciprocates your love and compassion and only tries to gain an advantage over you by manipulating your feelings, it is time to take a call. A relationship that is one sided has no future.

Look at Your Own Actions

Although the other person may be the problem, you need to also look at your own actions. This can enable you to gain clarity and you may be able to look at things in a new perspective. If you had suffered from an unhealthy family relationship, then toxic relationships may look normal and therein lies the problem.

When you start looking at things in a different manner, you may be able to discuss the issues openly with your family member and may be able to salvage the situation. If there is still no improvement in their behavior, you need to think how you are going to deal with this relationship.

Distance Yourself and Make the Cut

If possible, distance yourself completely from your toxic family member. Limit your interactions with them, so that they are not able to manipulate you in any way. Although all of us want to maintain cordial relationships with our family members, it may not always be possible to do so.

If, despite your best efforts, the relationship with your family member continues to go downhill, you need to make the difficult choice of cutting them completely from your life. Family is important but it should not be at the cost of your own physical and emotional well-being.

Limit Collateral Damage

The unfortunate thing about dealing with toxic family members is that when you sever all ties with one member it can affect others, too. You may be made to feel guilty and held responsible for breaking up a loving family. Be prepared to lose other relationships too.

Before you decide to deal with a toxic family member, it is best to talk with others in the family so that they are aware of the situation. This can help limit the collateral damage. Setting boundaries may be difficult but you do need to remember that you are doing this for your own good.

Be Cordial

Although you may want to avoid any kind of contact with your toxic family member, you are most likely to run into them at family gatherings. Be cordial to avoid difficult situations. Having a good support system can make it easier.

Always remember that fighting hatred and anger with hatred may only complicate things further. When you hold on to grudges you may not be able to recover from the pain you suffered. Forgive and move on.

When you end a relationship with a toxic family member, it can cause a lot of emotional upheaval. It is normal to feel guilt, anger, resentment and loneliness. You need to accept that it is going to be tough. Remember that you need to be happy too.

Chapter 4

Toxic Relationships at Workplace

Most of us begin our careers passionate and eager for growth with a chance to use our unique skills in a friendly environment. How do we end up cynical, depressed and stressed out? Why are we in a bad mood so often? Why do we distrust and fear our colleagues and boss? The answer to all these questions is that you are working in a toxic workplace.

The most common reasons that workplaces become toxic include poor management practices, ongoing conflicts, personal agendas and unresolved emotional issues at work. How do you know if your working environment is toxic?

1. Low Morale and High Stress

There is little joy or enthusiasm in what you do at the workplace. You are in a bad mood at all times, leading to chronic high stress. The culture of bullying and fear at the workplace can result in low morale.

2. Increase in Emotional and Physical Illness

Individuals working in toxic work environments have problems with their personal health. The physical symptoms may include insomnia, obesity, cardiovascular diseases and other similar problems. Emotional symptoms include depression, anxiety, mood swings, anger and irritability.

Why have you changed so much? Are you stressed? Do you want to talk about anything at the workplace? You know that you are having issues at the workplace when your family and friends start bringing things to your notice.

When your personal relations are impacted due to negativity at the workplace, it is sure sign of a toxic work environment. You are so stressed at the workplace that you stop paying attention to what is happening in your personal life.

3. Lack of Work-Life Balance

Do you feel that your organization wants to own you? Do you work long hours each week? Does your work cut into your family commitments? If you are forced to choose between having a job and having a life, it is a clear sign of a toxic workplace.

All of us need to have work-life balance and if your workplace makes you feel guilty about having a life, you need to get out of such a toxic environment. This can be dangerous to your emotional and mental health.

4. Poor Communication

Lack of communication or poor communication is often a telltale sign of a toxic workplace. If there is a significant communication problem across various areas like employer and employees, management and employees, management and different departments and even customers and suppliers, it is an initial sign of a dysfunctional workplace.

You are never kept in the loop and do not know what is going on at the workplace. If the only feedback you get from your employer is negative irrespective of what you did, then you are working in an environment that is toxic.

5. Immature Leaders

Toxic workplaces are often characterized by dysfunctional and immature leaders. These leaders are high on bullying, intimidation and aggression as they want to instill fear in others.

They are unwilling to listen to others and have unreasonable goals and expectations. Immature leaders are cold and emotionally distant. They are hypocritical and do not walk the talk.

6. Dysfunctional Relationships

The various dysfunctional dynamics at the workplace include favoritism, backbiting, insincere communication, holding grudges for long and pitting team members against each other. Instead of teamwork and unity a toxic workplace has a clique of outsiders and insiders.

7. Blaming Others

The mistakes are always blamed on others. The employees are constantly belittled. Even high performing employees are criticized for incompetence. Bullies are tolerated and admired. The entire department may be intimidated by bullies and management may lack expertise on how to deal with this situation.

How to Cope with Toxic Work Environment

Like life, work also has its ups and downs. The atmosphere at the workplace can affect your life in more ways than one and if you are not careful, you may soon be walking physically and emotionally ill to work.

Negative people at the workplace can take a toll on your health and sanity. As they are part of your everyday routine at work you may not be able to avoid them completely. Most people are demoralized and lose their passion for work when they stay long in a toxic work environment.

If your job is causing you serious physical and emotional stress, you need to get out as early as possible. But if you decide to stay, there are various ways that you can cope with toxic colleagues, boss and manager.

Distance Yourself

Putting a physical distance with a toxic individual at a workplace may not be possible, as you have to share work space. Although physical distance may not work, you can distance yourself emotionally and mentally from the toxic individuals influence.

Set boundaries and make them clear to those working with you. If the toxic individual crosses the boundaries that you have set and behaves in a manner that is inappropriate, you can make a complaint to your manager or boss.

If you are having trouble with your boss or manager, you need to talk with them to sort the tricky issues. Whatever it is, you do need to remember that it is not your fault.

Maintain Positivity

One of the most effective ways to cope in a toxic work environment is to maintain positive at all times. Although this is easier said than done, you may be able to counter negativism only with positivity.

Make a conscious decision that you will maintain positivity even when facing difficult situations. Spend more time with colleagues and coworkers that are constructive and happy. This can be a simple but effective way to counterbalance toxic behavior at the workplace.

Clear Misunderstandings

Do not let the problems fester. Clear any misunderstanding you may have with your colleague or manager immediately in a professional manner. Most problems at the workplace happen due to lack of communication.

If you do not confront any issues you may have at the workplace immediately and let them fester they may soon turn into something that you had not intended. This can contribute to an already prevailing toxic work environment and worsen things further.

Avoid drama and gossip, as they contribute immensely to misunderstandings at the workplace. It is advisable to focus on facts and not on gossip.

Protect Yourself

If you want to survive a toxic workplace, you need to protect yourself. The constant barbs and rants may have an emotional effect on any person and you are no exception. Talk with colleagues you can trust as this can lighten the situation.

Familiarize yourself with all policies and document everything. This can offer some kind of defense against managers and others intending to show you in bad light.

Be Assertive

If you want to maintain your sanity at the workplace, you may have to be assertive. If necessary, you may have to confront the person that is causing you grief. Although confrontations are not easy they may become necessary if abusive behavior at the workplace does not stop.

When you suffer in silence you embolden the person indulging in manipulative and abusive behavior. Most toxic individuals are cowards who tend to back off when confronted.

If your coping techniques are not getting you anywhere and the work environment has become unbearable, it is best to quit. This is the right decision especially if you are getting sick. When you work in a toxic workplace for long, you may start accepting bad behavior as normal.

One of the things that you need to realize is that you cannot control what people say and do but you can control what you say and do. When you are in complete control of your emotions, you may be able to deal better in a toxic work environment.

If nothing changes at the workplace even after you have tried all techniques of coping, you need to walk away with your head held high. It is important that you stop the harm before it starts affecting your capability and self-worth.

When you notice people caught in unhealthy situations, you fail to understand how they became caught in this vicious cycle. The fact is most people in such situations are blind to the reality and often live in the hope that things may change for the better.

Chapter 5

Smart Techniques for Handling Toxic People

Toxic people tend to defy logic and are usually blissfully unaware of the negative impact they have on others. They derive utmost satisfaction from pushing other people's buttons and creating chaos. Even when they come with warning signs around their necks, they may be difficult to avoid, as they are people you care for and love.

One of the best ways to handle toxic people is to manage your emotions and remain calm under pressure. If you want to effectively deal with such people, you need an approach that enables you to effectively control things that you can and discard those that you can't.

1. Ignore Attention Seekers

Toxic people seek attention at all costs. Even when it is your special day (birthday, anniversary or promotion), these people will make an effort to find a way to make it about them. They may usually begin with small actions such as interrupting others when they are talking to you or acting out or getting loud and obnoxious.

When they do not get the attention that they crave for their actions may become more drastic. They may start throwing a tantrum or start arguments and act in a destructive manner. Things may become truly ugly when they try and harm you.

The best course of action is to stay calm and pay little or no attention to the troublemaker. When you ignore the attention seekers long enough they tend to get the message that they are not going to get the attention they crave and may eventually stop behaving badly.

2. Set Limits

Negative people wallow in self-pity and want people to join the pity party and feel sad for them. This makes them feel better about themselves. Most of us feel pressure to listen to complainers, as we do not want to be perceived as rude.

You do need to remember that there is a thin line that separates lending a sympathetic ear and getting sucked into negativity. Avoid this by setting limits and distancing yourself from negative people.

A simple way to deal with constant complainers is to ask them how they are going to find a solution to their problems. When you start focusing on the solution instead of the problem, they may either change the conversation or quiet down.

Set limits or establish boundaries in a conscious and proactive manner. This ensures that you are in control of the situation. When you are in control the behavior of toxic people is much easier to predict and understand.

3. Avoid Manipulative People

Manipulative people may ruin your life. They can callously manipulate your feelings and make you say and do things that further their own individual goals. They can drive you crazy, as their behavior is irrational. If you want to avoid such people, you need to first recognize the signs of manipulation.

Do you feel unstable and strong emotions such as anger, resentment, irritation and sadness when they are around? Do you feel the need to explain everything to them? Are you made to feel inferior whatever you do?

Most people who manipulate others do so in such a subtle manner, you may hardly recognize that you have been manipulated against your own will. Remember that you do not need to justify, explain and make excuses to please anyone.

Be compassionate, understanding, respectful and kind to yourself. Reject behavior and requests that are turning you into something that you are not. If you find anyone toying with your emotions, it is best to avoid them.

4. Stand up to Bullies

This is one of the most effective ways of dealing with toxic people. Stand up to bullies, irrespective of who they are. They can be a family member, colleague, boss or your partner. Bullying can be both emotional and physical.

Toxic individuals tend to prey on those they consider weak and vulnerable. They take advantage of anyone they think may not be able to stand up to their bullying.

It is important that you stand up to these bullies not just for yourself but for others too.

When you stand up to a bully they are forced to change as they realize that they *may not have their way with you anymore.*

5. Stay Aware of Your Emotions

When you become aware of your emotions, you may be able to maintain a distance from the toxic individual. If you are not aware of what is happening, you may not be able to put an end to it.

Toxic people often put on a mask of helplessness so that they can manipulate your emotions. You need to decide that you will not be someone else victim. Remember that dealing with such people requires a lot of energy and will power.

6. Understand the Cycle and Pattern of Toxic Behavior

Toxic people tend to follow a particular pattern and cycle when dealing with others. Initially they are charming, attentive, impressive and loving, and this is primarily done to win your love and trust. When they become aware of your strengths and weaknesses they start manipulating you as per their needs.

You feel stuck and are unsure whether to give in to their demands or resist. You may feel compromised, as you do what they want. The problem is once you give in, it never stops.

You may be able to break this cycle of behavior only when you become aware of it. When you start understanding the pattern, you may be able to build boundaries that do not allow yourself to be fooled by any kind of behavior.

7. Don't Need Their Approval

Never look for appreciation or approval from toxic people. You need to remember that approval and appreciation only comes with conditions and you may feel drained when you give everything and get nothing back in return.

Most people tend to give in to toxic people in their life with the hope that they may get back something in return. Develop a network of people that are trustworthy and loyal, so that you do not have to depend on negative people for everything.

Do not allow anyone to restrict your happiness. You need to be the master of your own happiness and celebrate what you have successfully accomplished in life.

Although it is not realistic to be happy at all times in a relationship, you do not have to justify why you are not happy anymore. Remember that you may not be the problem. Happiness should be a mutual feeling.

If you want to deal with toxic people successfully, you need to identify the weakness in your approach. You may have to tap into your support system, so that you may be able to gain perspective of the challenges that you may face when dealing with such individuals.

Ask for assistance when you need it. Identify individuals who may be able to assist you and get a new perspective. Your support system may be able to see a solution when you can't, as they are not emotionally involved with the toxic individual.

One of the things that always offers hope when dealing with toxic relationships is that people change. There are some relationships that can be repaired if the individual had been indulging in negative behavior due to physical or mental illness. In such situations, you need to find the strength to hang on and put in the effort to keep things intact.

You need to understand that you may be a contributing factor to their toxic behavior. Ask yourself what needs to be changed and then make the change. Remember that people are not born toxic and it is usually circumstances and the environment that makes them who they are. Try and see the good in a person behaving negatively.

Focus on the positive characteristics of the individual instead of focusing on the negative aspects. Although it is difficult to do this when you are hurt and angry, it is advisable to make an effort, if you value the relationship.

When you have invested a lot in a relationship, you may not be willing to accept that you are in a toxic relationship. Acceptance is really important to start the healing process. Unless you accept the reality, you may not be able to change yourself or the person behaving in a negative manner.

Real life relationships are no fairy tale. They take a lot of hard work to stay strong.

Chapter 6

Strategies for Dealing with Toxic People

Surviving the ups and downs of living with a toxic individual can be quite a challenge. One of the important things that you need to remember is that these people may also be going through a difficult phase. They may be chronically worried, ill or lack emotional support.

Irrespective of the reasons for their behavior, dealing with negative people is never easy. As toxic individuals manipulate and intimidate you, inflicting enduring abuse and misery, it may take a bit of an effort to regain your self-esteem and confidence.

1. Stop Pretending Toxic Behavior is Acceptable

If you are not careful, toxic individuals may make use of their manipulative nature to get preferential treatment. Most of us think that it is much easier to give in to their demands than hear them complaining. You need to understand that these people prey off the energy of others.

They are usually so discreet in what they do that they do not get caught. Even when you are able to identify the pattern of their toxic behavior they know exactly what to say and do and try to wriggle out of the situation.

If you find yourself constantly making excuses for their behavior or reason for their actions, it means that they have complete control over your emotions. This creates a cycle where you are constantly giving in to their demands.

You may think that you are getting out of a short-term problem but the fact is that you are creating a long-term problem. When they learn how to manipulate your feelings they make use of this information to make you do whatever they want.

Toxic individuals may never change their behavior if you keep rewarding them for not changing. You need to decide that you will not be influenced by their behavior. Negativity and constant drama is not something that you need to put up with. Take a stand and stop pretending that you will accept toxic behavior.

2. Move on and Delete Toxic People from your Environment

If a person close to you deliberately insists on destroying your emotional state of mind, you need to understand that they are toxic. Are you suffering because of their attitude? Does your compassion and patience only seem to aggravate the situation? You need to ask yourself, "Do I need this individual in my life?".

Although you may care about the individual, you need to decide whether you need them in your life. When you remove toxic people from your environment, you may be able to regain control of your life. If possible, you need to move on without them. You need to decide enough is enough and be strong.

A healthy relationship is reciprocal as it involves give and take but when you are caught in a toxic relationship, you only give and receive nothing but pain and heartbreak. No healthy relationship can survive in such a scenario.

When you let go of toxic people from your life, it does not mean that you hate them or that you wish them any kind of harm. It only means that you care your health and well-being and that you want to be happy.

3. Stand Up for Yourself

Toxic individuals will do anything for their own personal gain. They will belittle and bully you, make you feel guilty and cause anger and resentment. Do not accept such behavior.

You may be surprised to know that most toxic people know that what they are doing is wrong but as they always seem to get away with such behavior they keep repeating it. As they gain an upper hand during such situations they continue causing trouble.

When confronted these people back down. When you speak up they will keep quiet. Toxic individuals often use anger as a tool to influence and intimidate you. They may avoid responding to you when you communicate with them or start talking negatively about someone you love.

It is important that you confront them when they indulge in such negative behavior. They may be initially surprised when you speak up and respond in an aggressive manner but it is important that you stand up to them.

When you start challenging their behavior, you may get them to realize the negative impact they are having on your emotions and life. Be direct, as this can open a door of opportunity for you to make them understand the seriousness of the problem.

Even when they deny that they are in the wrong, you can be happy that you have made them realize their mistake. Most people cannot be in denial forever and may have to accept their behavior and make amends. There are some individuals who may never accept that they are wrong and it is futile to spend time and effort on them.

When an individual does not change even after you confront and stand up to him/her, it is best to eliminate them from your life if possible. If you are not able to do so you can restrict the time spent with them.

4. Find the Strength to Defend Yourself

Your dignity and self-esteem may be attacked and you may be mocked but you need to remember that no one can claim victory over you unless you willingly surrender. You need to find your inner strength to defend yourself.

You have to demonstrate that you will not be belittled and intimidated. Give a clear message that you are no longer willing to participate in their mind games. When you do not give in to their abusive behavior and show that you are willing to stand up and defend yourself they may back off.

Negative people only attack those that they feel are helpless. When you constantly give in to their manipulations it gives them the power to take control of your life. When you start setting boundaries and make an effort to defend yourself, you regain the confidence and self-esteem that was eluding you.

Do not let anyone judge or criticize you for the way you look and behave. Never change because your partner says so as it can ruin your self-confidence. Most negative people use all their charms to make you do things that they want and you may require a lot of inner strength to say no.

5. Practice Compassion

Does it make sense to be sympathetic towards toxic individuals? The answer of this question is a resounding "YES". Although it may be difficult to show compassion and love to people that you are angry with, it is advisable to make a start.

People who indulge in toxic behavior are not necessarily bad. These individuals may be suffering from an illness or they may be going through a difficult time. Some individuals may be genuinely depressed or distressed and these issues may be prompting them to behave in a certain manner.

You do need to remember that if you let people get away with bad behavior because they are depressed or suffering from an illness they may subconsciously start using these circumstances for their own benefit. If you want the relationship to be saved you need to make an effort.

Be compassionate towards toxic individuals, but at the same time you need to set boundaries. When you keep forgiving them for their mistakes and allow them to do whatever they want, you may never be able to bring a positive change in their nature. Be compassionate but firm and make it clear that you will not tolerate any kind of toxic behavior anymore.

6. Take Time to Relax and Recuperate

You need to take time for yourself when forced to work or live with toxic individuals. If you do not take time to relax and recuperate, the toxic behavior may affect your emotional and physical well-being. Your emotional state of mind can have a big effect on your physical body.

Sleep well and talk to friends. Remember that you need the time to live in a peaceful manner away from toxic behavior. You learn how to deal with things in a positive manner when you take time for yourself. This usually has a great effect on your individuality even if it is not immediate.

7. Don't Take Toxic Behavior Personally

Always remember that is it them and not you. Negative individuals may always try and imply that you have done something wrong. They want you to feel guilty, as this gives them the power to intimidate and manipulate you as per their wishes.

They know that when we start feeling guilty we blame no one but us for the situation. We think that we have done something wrong and this can have a big impact on our self-esteem and confidence. Do not let this happen to you.

Avoid feeling guilty for something that you have not done. Don't get sucked into the guilt trap by taking everything personally. When you stop taking things personally, you feel a huge sense of freedom.

Toxic individuals behave in a negative manner, not just with you, but with others too. Even when the situation is personal and you are directly belittled and insulted, you should remember that you are not responsible for the situation.

What negative people do and say has got nothing to do with you. When you start understanding this it enables you to look at things in a new perspective. You are able to stop the blame game and gain control over your emotions and life.

The most important thing that you need to remember when you are in a toxic relationship is that you are in control of things more than you realize. When you start implementing these healthy strategies for dealing with toxic people, you may be able to slowly train your brain to handle such situations in a better manner.

With time, you become more positive and proactive in your approach. Be quick to forgive but do not forget. When you forgive, you are letting go of what happened to you and you move on. This does not mean that you are giving the toxic individual another chance. You may stop feeling guilty when you forgive.

When you let go of things, you ensure that you are not bogged down by other people's mistakes. This simple assertion helps protect you from future harm. When you learn the skills to neutralize toxic behavior in individuals, you are a winner.

It is not easy to pick up the pieces after a toxic relationship as the pain is overwhelming. You may not be able to control all the things that toxic relationships do to you but you can decide that you will not be an emotional wreck in the long run. Decide that you will not let the actions of a toxic individual dictate your life.

In a perfect world, we may not have to deal with toxic relationships but we do not live in a perfect world. Decide whom to walk beside and whom to leave behind. This is your life.

Conclusion

Thank you again for downloading this book!

I hope this book was able to help you realize why you need to get out of a toxic relationship.

The next step is to use the techniques and strategies that are listed in the book for a happier life detoxed of all unhealthy relationships.

Finally, if you enjoyed this book, would you be kind enough to leave a review for this book on Amazon? Every review counts!

Thank you and good luck!

www.ingramcontent.com/pod-product-compliance
Lightning Source LLC
Chambersburg PA
CBHW060225290526
45789CB00003B/1415